Introduction

This book is a compilation of spoken word poems, traditional poems, and songs composed during my free time. It draws inspiration from the vibrant artistic community of Chicago and my poetry team at Fort Pierce Central High School.

In 2015, I participated in Louder Than A Bomb Florida during my senior year, which marked my introduction to spoken word poetry. Before that, I had been experimenting with music and rap. Writing has been a long-standing passion of mine, ignited during my freshman year of high school when my friend Brandon Mercado introduced me to influential lyricists like MF DOOM, Logic, and Ali Tomineek. My interest in poetry deepened in my sophomore year, largely due to my English teacher's poetry prompts and encouragement.

I joined Louder Than A Bomb Florida after learning about it from Timothy Davenport, a friend and fellow poet. Our team performed exceptionally well, reaching the finals and securing a fourth-place finish at the state level. This achievement led me to travel to Chicago, where I had the privilege of attending workshops with renowned poets such as Kevin Coval, Fatimah Asghar, Jamila Woods, Nate Marshall, and Malcolm London. Through these experiences, I learned the value of storytelling in spoken word poetry, which allows poets to connect with audiences who may share similar experiences or interests.

The collection includes songs that stem from imagination, curiosity, and a reflection of the world around us. While not all the pieces tackle serious themes, each holds personal significance for me. Louder Than A Bomb, initiated by Kevin Coval, has roots in the 1960s, emerging from the Underground Black Community. It was shaped by the Poetry and Political Music Group known as The Last Poets, who used their art to convey political messages and societal frustrations during the civil rights movement. Spoken word poetry serves as a powerful vessel for sharing stories of triumphs and addressing pressing societal issues. I utilize poetry not only as a form of expression and protest against injustices but also as a means of coping with various experiences in my life. May Poetry Never Die.
— Charles Evans

Table of contents
- **Freedom Writer**
- **Graduated**
- **Chicago**
- **Origins**
- **Words Pierce**
- **Equality**
- **New World**

- **Intertwined Hearts**
- **Dear Dad**
- **Equinox-(Tonka Poem)**
- **My love shines through(Acrostic Poem)**
- **The wise old man was loyal-(Acrostic Poem)**
- **My Journey**
- **The rights of the people**
- **Suicide**

Freedom Writer

I Am A Freedom Writer

This Movement is a religion to us,

Black and white will become a better mixture

Racism will be left in the dust,
For I have seen the world
Break The Chains of segregation
I've seen the truth through the ways of meditation,
Our world will crumble and fall if we keep spreading this hate
So put the guns down put your hands to the heavens,
We need love not all these other weapons,
So, tell me Why Does Skin Tone Matter?
We have our differences but is it fair that whites get away with making the pens?
And the Black community serve the sentences?
Not All cops are bad but why are the ones that decide to murder, Praise?
Killing with no evidence
Acting like they are heaven-sent,
Are we Blind to the real villains?
The government has armored cars and bodyguards but what are they protecting?
I'm not saying we should forget I'm just saying we should be accepting.
We should spread love we are all family, and we share the same blood
This is destined, for we all share the same blessings,
Welcome to the land full of energy, in the end, we will all have our victory, we have discriminated against each other for so many centuries.

I look back into history and see powerful black stories that have changed the world, The King had a dream and I have mine. Rosa sat on the front of the bus to receive her rights, so tell me is it wrong or right that just because of skin tone access is denied?

A world full of darkness I'm just trying to shine some light,

a poem about freedom here we go, we saw the Jim Crow and segregation laws under a bald eagle,

a place where the government is against its people, where money and power are true evil, I'll Walk into the problems with my hands high with your people,

in a world that is so unequal.

I'm sorry I don't see the world in black and white, I guess your eyes aren't as vivid as mine, I'm Colorblind, That's why I'm going to need you to remember me,

Just an 18-year-old kid spitting rhymes about what we need,

Break The Chains,

Poetry is my way to make a change,

what a source of irony,

The beautiful mixture of ebony and ivory because the ocean can't be without land,

This world will be free when all races come together hand in hand.

Graduated

This is how it feels to be Graduated

No more Infatuation

I remember smoking green

No more power cleans, No more

I remember the same projector screen

I remember the same whiteboard

I thought it would never happen

I was told I was never going to make it

Look at me now

Graduated

Footprints on the paper turned to shooting for stars

Talking about papers and stars

Look at Kobe from the Lakers he shot 'till he hit Mars

No more school food or chilling with the four dudes at about noon

No more being tired of that tiring classroom

I thought I was never going to make it

Look at me now

Graduated

Working Nine to Five

I remember waking up at Five

Brushing my teeth

Gotta make sure my clothes neat

Everybody is in line for the next trend

I was in line to meet up with my friends

The only high part about school was Cloud Nine and acting like fools

That time I got bent

After prom at the after party wishing it was never over

Because that aftermath of knowing that all of us were going our separate ways hit me

My poetry came in handy when I needed that extra hand because my hands weren't handy.

I remember Chicago with that sack full of some Hebru Brantley

I remember my friends who were band geeks,

Thought I hated it

Look at me now

Graduated

Never thought I would love school

That one last party at the pool

Where there were no Rules

Who knew what it could do because school was beautiful too, wish it was cleaner, I miss being a Senior.

I miss passing out Dumb Stupid

I Still Make Music

I thought I hated it

Look at me now

Graduated

Chicago

In the beautiful city of Chicago, a young poet was inspired.

Inquired

To transpire

To make a change

To see the beauty in every form of art

To see the beauty within the pain

To see the beauty within the words,

The young poet was inspired.

People who only have 2 hands can't paint a picture of a million words, so I lend my words to the people, I lend every toe and every finger, I lend a whole arm-length span because poetry taught me to give a helping hand.

Poetry

My passion

Satisfaction

Gave half of my life to it

So, this is more than just a fraction.

In the beautiful city of Chicago, I learned that at the end of the day, all poets just want to be loved, and every poet has love for one another, After a slam, I'll be glad to call these poets my brothers, A family tree,

A poet,

A Poet tree

We all came from poetry.

We all form our metaphors and similes into beautiful structures.

A trip that guaranteed him

That he would be something

After everyone told him he would be nothing

We save every ounce of strength in our veins to get on stage and spit lands of freedom.

In the beautiful city of Chicago

Where all arts form beautiful replicas of every imagination Where everywhere you turn is a beautiful creation, Creation, the stimulation of becoming yourself,

Finding that self-worth that kept you living, breathing, writing, creating,

Finding One's Purpose

In the beautiful city of Chicago

Origins

Where I am from sometimes people don't need a reason to stay but you find yourself searching for words to say because you're so scared of being replaced.

Where I am from you don't understand the feeling of hurt but you don't understand the worth, you understand it when you're speaking your last words.

Where I am from breathing is simple, I understand my body and treat it as a temple.

Where I am from the last time is never the last time, like do you remember the last time you said this was the last time? I'm finally getting over the past Time.

Where I am from It's not about falling in love with someone through things sexual, but respect and falling in love with someone through features so intellectual.

Where I am from, if the feelings are real, they should be unconditional, relationships shouldn't be so difficult, finding something true is blissful but is hard like math too, happiness under theirs like reciprocals just to find pieces of you.

Where I am from my mother said to be what you want to be, so where I am from, I am trying to turn my daydreams into reality,

Where I am from everything is vital, I feel smothered because my daydreams are always on standby leaving me to ask who am I and why are my dreams on idle.

Our purpose can't be the same, where I am from, we all try to find the purpose of why we were made.

Where I am from you learn to show less of yourself until you earn that respect because sometimes you feel disrespected and neglected too,

Where I am from, I'm surrounded by people who confuse chemistry with the energy of the vibes through intimacy just to feel the same frequencies, just because you share the same vibes doesn't mean you are meant to be.

Where I am from people generate lies and portray disguises just to penetrate your thighs. Where I am from people are so scared of letting go and stop pressing rewind like a VCR tape instead of moving forward like pressing play.

Where I am from letting go is hard, we're all afraid of breaking our hearts, all afraid of the nightmares, you can't live life being scared, misery comes for a reason and sometimes it's for the better, easier to stand, like Peter we are scared of growing up so we try to make our own little Neverlands.

Where I am from, we all want success, no matter if it's six or seven, we are all trying to make it, confidence will be the way to the efforts of making it to heaven, always praising but we already have our blessing, as our destiny beckons.

Where I am from, we all want what's in our hearts, we keep it in our eyes, when that fire dies, we finally realize what we lost, we are all lost causes trying to find our purpose, so Where I am from, I will continue writing until the change of this world surfaces.

Words Pierce

See they say fake it until you make it but what happens if I keep faking till my mind goes blank and I can no longer write these words on this damn page,

Until I lost my only escape, poetry was my way to make a change and I've spoken poetry about breaking the chains of segregation, I've spoken poetry about the truths in the ways of meditation,

I've spoken poetry, poetry about love but what happens when poetry finally loses my trust, because my life lately has been feeling torturous,

I miss the days when poetry would cast those ever-so-deep metaphorical spells on me like a sorcerous,

How about that day when my grandpa died in my arms because the only time that I don't feel like I'm in solitary confinement is when I'm speaking behind these damn bars.

So, what happens when you're so worried about your clothes, you finally get so high to only realize you just hit your low?

See I know I should smoke a little less but I drown myself in smoke within these bars and I'm not talking cigarettes.

I remember when I was handing out my mixtapes on CD Roms, but I found my escape and HeRo encouraged me through louder than a bomb and I remember all my team because they were on my back I swear I was weird but I still rep the fact that words pierce,

I'm just trying to be a little bit more outspoken like a character in a glitch saying Broken game, broken game broken game, because poetry was my way to make a change,

I remember that relation with that dope house over there don't go over there, or how about being a child of just another statistic because those three girls were the only hope left for their father

See changing the world with words is an ease,

I know what it's like to lose a grandparent from a disease because I hate cancer too,
I remember being 14 and nobody noticing the tear stains on my glasses, and I remember I would daydream in classes and think about why my tears were clear if all that water was just coming from deep inside, and yes even though I'm on the outside looking in I know nobody should take that pride from your roots because when they tell you to put your hands up I say nah stand up because all I was told was I don't want to hear a word but words are the gateway for others to learn.

    So, what happens when I can no longer turn to writing for support? I turn to my team in the fort because you guys have helped me through so much and just know after looking countless times and places I have found you.

.

Equality

Bullets with bullets falling to the ground while the police load their next rounds for the next black victims, I'm tired of all these ignorant states of mind, talking about who isn't, he had a gun, that's no excuse, social neglection to the truth, whites are carefree while the blacks are still getting abused, he had a gun, but that gun was put away, so when is the change going to come before another corrupt pig gets away, I don't usually talk on pork, usually don't have beef what's up with the police.

I don't want to hear that all lives matter we are looking to move forward, to keep climbing the ladder, we have to hit the top,

I'm glad my momma raised me right growing up, because she taught me that race doesn't matter, but not much of us had that luck, America the home of the great, protected by the brave, take it back hold up the clouds are getting grey, none of this is right, these cops are hiding behind millimeters of nine, see I can't mess with this world because it's either you are a racist or hateful it's either you hate it or your grateful, a black and white world with a bitter taste, what happened to the world that was tasteful?

Some of these people don't want to be great

Some of these people just want to see hate

Some of your friends want to be fake

Some of your families are going to be snakes

Feeling so funny I don't want to see straight,

We are looking at a world full of genocide

Instead of a world full of children's smiles

Funny days with sunny rays

Speak the truth you're villainized

Countless innocents keep dying

Speaking out loud for Palestine

Baby's getting killed mothers crying

Americas going insane

Inside jobs money to Ukraine

Being taxed out of our asses, governments to blame

I grew up with my best friend, white and black hand in hand, I remember back when classrooms were full of white and black and we all got along,

Maybe that's why I'm making this poem to bring a little bit of peace,
anything can happen as fast as a rustle in the leaves.
So, I'm down to act like a hooligan
In a movement like a missionary to Jerusalem,
Seven sins and only one deadly Keeping my pen ready to write down everything I see Trying to bring this world some peace

New World

It's a sad world oh yes, it is
It's a sad world save the kids Build a new world
We just want to live

We can't even feed the needy. Help those in pain Inside jobs Send money to Ukraine United as one Take back the power or be like sheep and Watch TV and cower.
It's a sad world oh yes, it is
It's a sad world let's save the kids
Build a new world
We just want to live

   We Can't even speak opinions Without getting shut down or Being called racist because they tried it in a small town We need to settle down and Realize We are not enemies in a world full of people We're fed greed and envy We live in a world where they keep on tempting and trying us A world ran by people in control of dividing us.
It's a sad world oh yes, it is
It's a sad world save the kids

Bring a new world

We just want to live

Every day's A splinter of time Being wasted away While we sit,

laugh a little and embrace our mind's Geometry in lines.

One body spirit and mind

Good soldiers all died but what did they die for, this world becoming

so cold Due to dystopian molds

Never want the thought of rejection

Only the thought of acceptance

Always complain about depression

you can change your perception through meditation and reach

elevation

Everybody wants change but nobody changes so

Everybody wants to be happy but can't stand the pain though

It's easier to reject accountability than to find someone to blame so

What are we doing here

We have kids on the street

Systematic racism

Making it illegal to speak

Families not able to eat

Never trust another

Betrayal from my brother

Being done like Cain did Abel

I grab the umbrella for the next day man

Lies pouring on me like rain from the Rainmen

I try to spread love through my messages

Music has been my only therapy session

Helping me through my depression

Feeling this energy hitting like excellence

Got my DNA upgrades from the resonance

I would not beef with me

Check the Schumann frequency

Earth we were not expecting this

Wish I wasn't dreaming

Waking up screaming

Like a banshee

Separating the posers with my flow so atrocious like I'm Moses

And the Red Sea

I keep my energy so divine

Call it synergy

We got positive vibes

ancient geometry in our mind

Forming symmetry with every line

I put passion into every rhyme

I meditate to elevate my mind

Feeling so sublime

Uncover truth feeling alive

Born in the darkness

Rose To the light

A glitch in the matrix

Corporations started this hatred

Mix some determination with the flame, another level

I'm just a soul attached to this vessel

I put passion into every lyric

They counted me out

They didn't want to hear it

Fought through my storms

The perseverance

Didn't give a fuck about my appearance

Cheap shoes but wealthy with lyrics

On this journey

It's been eccentric

Keep my soul in touch,

I found my spirit

the devil can't come near it

I've chosen this as my vessel

I made it through the pain

my eyes have been tearing

Looking at my friends wondering if they hear me

Time away hurt me severely

I've been so exhausted and weary

But I love you sincerely

It's a sad world oh yes, it is

It's a sad world save the kids

Bring forth a new world We just want to live

Intertwined hearts

As I lay awake listening to the wind breeze,

The warmth of your smile

The look in your eyes will forever bring me to my knees

To you, I am just a man but for me, you are all I am and I cannot let that go

Inside a beast but outside a shell of a man

I will forever stay by your side even in the afterlife as our souls grow old.

Dear dad

Dear Dad, I hope to see you at my birthday next week All my teachers say I'm doing great in the 3rd grade doing college algebra, but the other kids call me a geek, all I ever wanted was a friend, oh yea my teacher gave me an umbrella because I was playing alone and mom has been busy every day on the phones but it had my favorite Spider-Man! Well, Dad, I hope you make it but tonight Mom got off early so she's going to read me a bedtime story from beginning to end.

Dear Dad, it's been 16 years since I've been alive and I still haven't heard from you, I wonder if you even know who I am, well you won't get this letter because I don't know where to send this.

Well, I've been writing more and more, I'm starting to get the hang of poetry, everyone says I suck at it but I try not to listen to them, I guess it just calms me down when I'm having my panic attacks, it's my calm through the storm when I cannot relax, and honestly, I need it.

Oh, Dad me and my friend Brandon I made what's called a mixtape where you rap to another artist's beat and we passed it out on a CD. Dear Michael, I thought about taking my life, my mom found me with cuts on my arms, and she confiscated all my knives, I don't know Dad I've just been feeling empty inside, I know you don't know me but when I'm at school I feel like I have to hide because I can't get the thought out of my mind of my cousin committing suicide, you didn't know her either she's not blood, but it hurts knowing you don't give a fuck to take five minutes out of your day and just check on your son, I feel like I'm half orphan, I mean come on dad am I even important? Why won't you just write to me? Why can't you just call? I feel like I'm going crazy within my head's walls,

I feel jailed in bars and those bars are these words because all I can ever write about anymore is just sad thoughts, am I crazy Dad?

Hey dad! I did it and I proved all of them wrong! I couldn't be more overly excited.

My poetry team and I were invited out to Chicago after our show and remember the old dolphin's player Jason Taylor? He said he's paying!!! I'm so happy I can't believe it, Dad my team was amazing and Lafayette, Tashona, Kayla, and Saiya, they killed it we were so relieved! I've been thinking Dad, my team's motto was words pierce but honestly what I think is worse is your silence…

Dear Dad, I haven't heard from you in a while. I hope you're okay, you know I got a message from a lady saying you were dead… I don't know what to say. I'm 23 now dad and I haven't even met you this can't be true there's no way I lost you; I haven't even met you yet but from what the obituary and your side of the family are saying you're dead, they invited me to the funeral dad I don't know what to say… They told me you didn't show up for work and someone called for a Welfare check. I've put all my love and effort into my art instead of checking up on you, I didn't know it was your heart, and I can't relax knowing I just lost my dad and grandfather from heart attacks. Dad my only wish was to meet you I've been so cold to everybody, I guess it was just me holding a grudge over myself for never meeting you, dad today is the first day I met your side of the family, I hate that I can't meet you, I love you dad aunt Thelma sent me pictures of me up on your shoulders when I was a baby, I had so many weird questions to ask you like did I get my sweet tooth from you for chips and sodas? Or hey Dad do you still have that Chevy Nova? Well, Dad… they say you must start with the man in the mirror, and from what all the townspeople say is true, Dad I'm going to make sure I'm a better-spitting image of you, dad I didn't realize how life could be so short, all the anger and depression I can't let it overtake me no more, so I promise today I'm going to do better and make people happy because you taught me one thing, love is the only thing that will keep this earth spinning around, and dad I just want to say I love you. Rest in peace Michael Evans.

Equinox-(Tonka Poem)

As the leaves rustle in the wind,

The sweet air brings back memories

Of times filled with laughter and joy

May the spring equinox begin again

As the cold melts away, spring begins another day

My love shines through (Acrostic Poem)

I

Leave my frustrations behind

Only when it is safe will I bring you close

Visible for now and all time

Every day it will remain alive

You are my everything

Only you will know

Under no circumstances will I ever let it die

As it will be and as it has been

Love will always guide you to me

Whether you become lost or in a mess

Along the way

You will find your way

So stay and don't let our love fade away

The wise old man was loyal-(Acrostic Poem)

Lonely in a room full of people
Observing the many personalities
Yellowing of bone teeth and greying of hair
Attentive to the youth playing
Longing for the joy of being young again.

My Journey

Growing up, I was always told I was supposed to be seen and not heard.

Little did I know I was meant to be heard, not just seen, you see sticks and stones may break your bones, but words, pierce your confidence.

That same kid who was told to be seen and not heard, the same kid who was told he would be nothing and turned his ambition into determination and rose

Through all the hardship, I learned to take a positive position in life.

You see, the world is just 2 sides, and that's dark and light
We see it in every religion, let me just mention it.
The Yin and Yang
Good comes from bad, and bad can come from good. See, I was just a poor kid coming from the hood,
2-bedroom apartment fitting five.
That was me.
As I got older, my cousin took her life and then came depression
I couldn't get past the waves as they kept crashing and drowning me, music and writing became my passion until it overstepped and became an obsession, being told I would never get anywhere, I gave up.
After the year of 2016, I wasn't a normal teen; my demons followed me How do you think a 17-year-old felt when he held his grandfather cold and dead in his hands? Ptsd now you see
It's funny because everyone has told me not to wear my heart on my sleeve
But I do because, quite frankly, I can not relax
At the age of 17, my grandfather died of a heart attack.
As they pumped and pumped to get him back, it was too late. His heart stopped beating on the way to the hospital.
This molded me.
I lived every day blaming myself for not being able to save him.
Then came along louder than a bomb, Florida,
I touched lives with words. It ended and Just to get by and pay bills I went straight to work putting down all my sweet satisfactions. One

being poetry but as time went on I knew my passion was formed into the poets tree, so I had a mission.

Now, every day, I help and change someone's life for the better.

Now you see I laid out my dice on the table and took a leap of faith not knowing I was able to be great. I was ready to give up ready to throw the towel in.

But I knew I had a mission, so I tied my demons away and let them submerge

Let this be a lesson

Do not let anyone tell you, you are only to be seen and not heard.

Because changing someone's life with your voice is your soul's expression through human connection.

The rights of the people

And for the politicians, if you're scared, I don't care that the power you took is a commitment, you should have thought about the corruption when you stood on 150 million Americans' First Amendment. You did this to yourselves, but looking at that bill it sounds like you're planning to imprison, so let's face it our founding fathers laid it out for us 27 amendments, a process of ratification, a loud voice, and commitment on top of a little persistence, we just trying to be left the alone not apart of the corporate business,

Didn't the common law say we have the right to the pursuit of happiness, life, and liberty?

Tell me, why do we have to go to war when we didn't even envision this, not to mention this is the 21st century? If you end it with nukes, there will be no existence, This world is Cold. A grandson of a soldier. I will not fold, built on perseverance,

A bill to lock me up for the martyr I'm becoming because I'll keep speaking through truth about corporate greed through poems like E.E. Cummings, and I didn't forget what you did to Tesla, the act of bad faith and greed mixed with hysteria, for sure the truth is coming It's fascinating, a 25-year-old kid ready to lead a nation, don't worry, I've already been looking over my shoulder asking when they will assassinate him for speaking the real truth and exposing the eradication.

Bipartisan support to ban an app, taking rights from the people, when did the government become the people's equal? What about all the kids who never made it home to their dads? This is why I can't relax, it's both sides of the party, left and right, you ban books on black history and want us to think it's not a direct attack? What about those kids in Texas who never got to leave their class? Do you not see you're creating your demise, evil intentions by passing bills to censor our speech, but banning an app that has no ties?

I think it's kind of funny, a hunter in hiding,

Sending money to funnel your son's business "expenses," what are you doing, Biden? Cocaine in the White House? No wonder you can't form a sentence,

You put millions of minorities away

Why isn't your son in prison?

Can't you see America is fed up

I'm an Aquarius trying to spread truth within my season, you politicians raised your right hand to take oath, and now all of you are committing treason, yes and I hope those words cut like a knife, infringing on these American's rights, I see the dollar collapsing and people going on like sheep, still under the facade and the mask of a tyrannical government criticizing and blasting anyone ready to speak.

All I ask is that if this causes protests, please be peaceful. I remember when my assistant principal said The pen defeats evil, the pen is mightier than the sword,

They're gonna call me crazy.

They'll try to put me in a ward, but I do this for we the people, stay peaceful, and protest without violence.

We are poets and will never be silenced.

Suicide

Secluded from reality

Under false hope

Is this what this life offers?

Can I bring myself to stay strong?

Is this all that I can do?

Does anyone hear me?

Everything I love has faded.

(This Poem is dedicated to my beautiful cousin Colleen Christine Owen. May you rest in peace, you will forever be loved. October 28th, 1989- November 8th, 2009)

From the Author: Some of these poems are experiences i have been through in life, some experiences are not as pleasant for others, it is not my mission to bring forth sadness or depression onto anyone, I want to make it clear though, in no way Am I suicidal, I have learned that life is amazing and there is much to offer from life, so if you are having a hard time please reach out to someone and talk to them, if you do not have anyone to reach out to please dial 1-800-273-TALK for suicide awareness hotline, It may have been converted to an easier number to dial being 988, This world has far to much to offer even when you are at your lowest point, Please Reach out. Make it acceptable to speak on your issues, as that is what spoken word poetry was made for. We are all poets who want to be loved.

Made in the USA
Columbia, SC
23 April 2025